HAL•LEONARD

GUITAR
PLAY-ALONG

AUDIO
ACCESS
INCLUDED

PLAYBACK+
Speed • Pitch • Balance • Loop

VOL. 52

FUNK

CONTENTS

To access audio visit:
www.halleonard.com/mylibrary

2337-8751-2075-1865

ISBN 978-1-4234-0055-4

HAL•LEONARD®
7777 W. BLUEMOUND RD. P.O. BOX 13819 MILWAUKEE, WI 53213

Visit Hal Leonard Online at
www.halleonard.com

Cissy Strut

By Arthur Neville, Leo Nocentelli, George Porter and Joseph Modeliste, Jr.

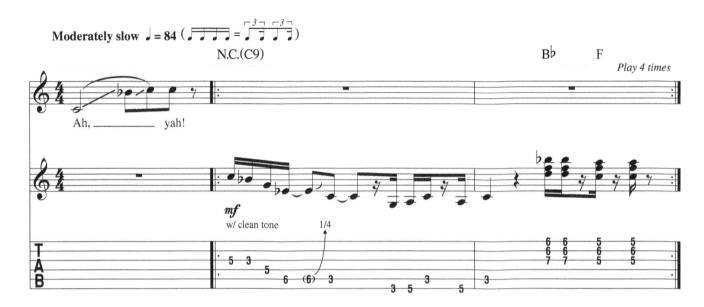

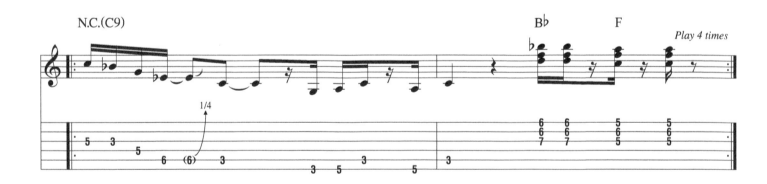

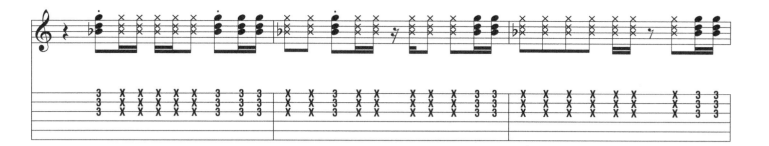

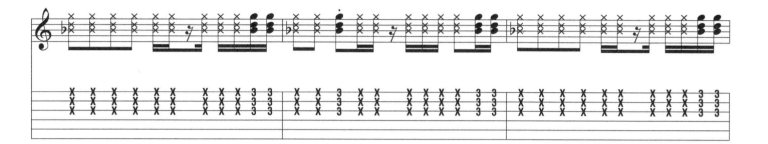

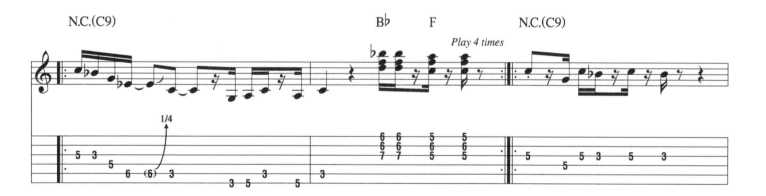

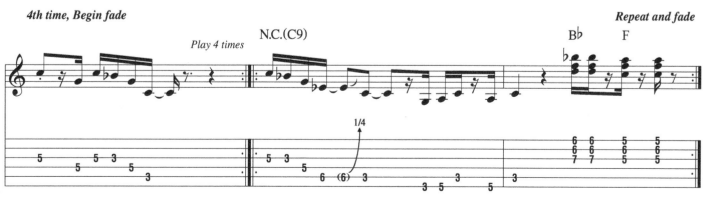

Flashlight

Words and Music by George Clinton Jr., William "Bootsy" Collins and Bernard G. Worrell

* Key signature denotes B Dorian.

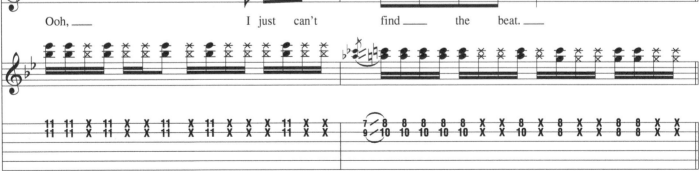

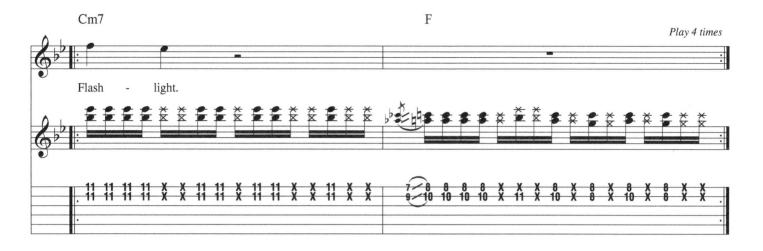

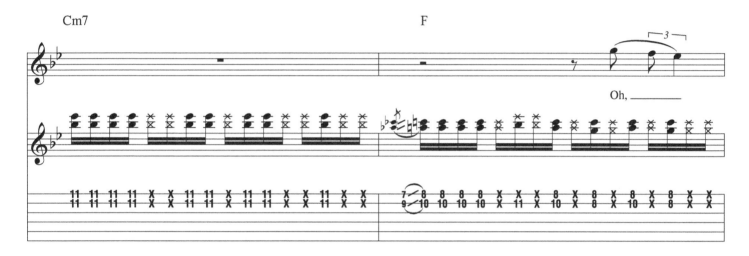

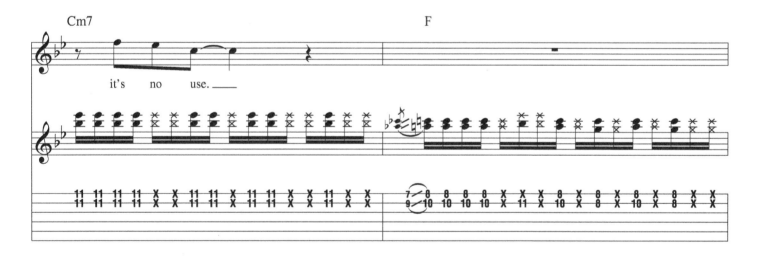

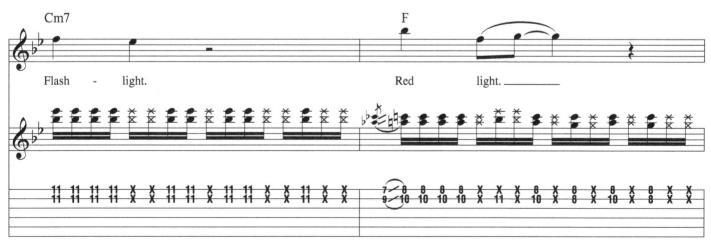

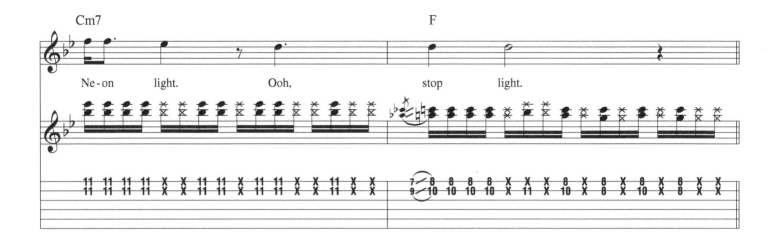

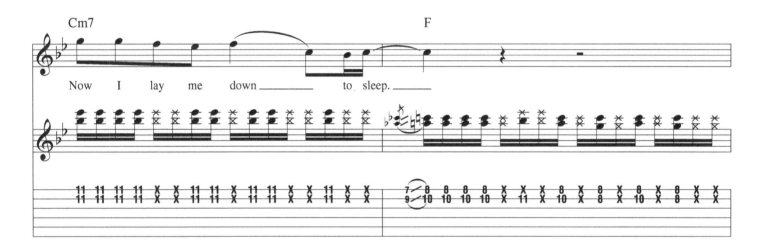

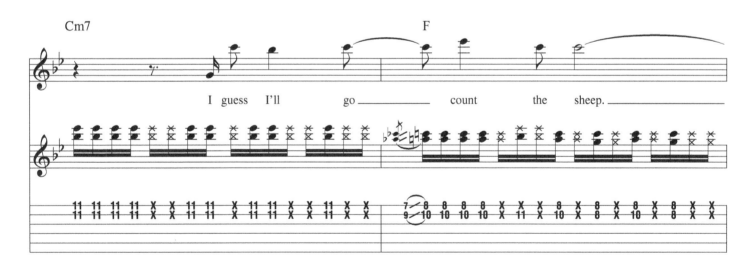

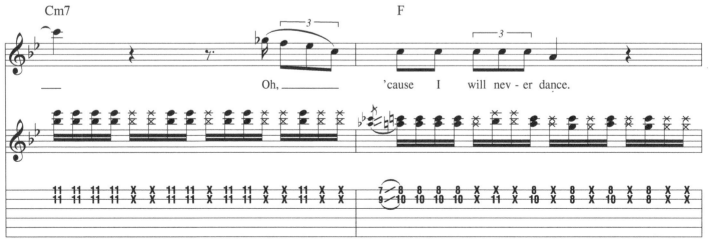

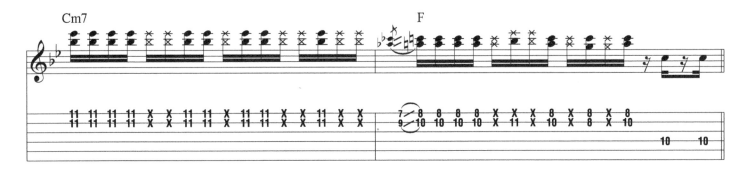

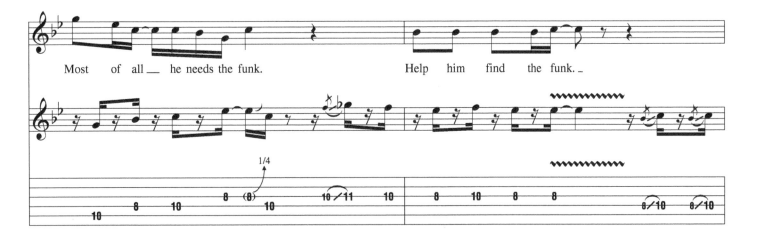

Most   of   all __   he needs the funk.   Help   him   find   the   funk. __

Most   of   all __   he needs the funk.   Help   him   find   the   funk. __

Most of all __ he needs the funk. Help him find the funk. __

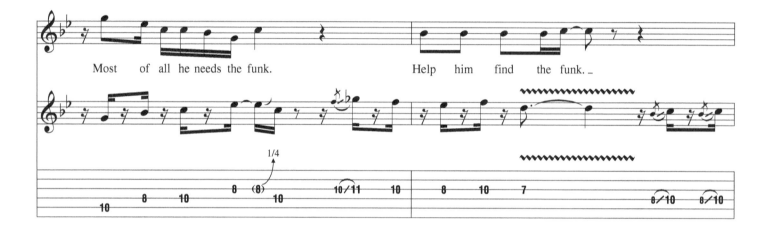

Most of all he needs the funk. Help him find the funk. __

Most of all __ he needs the funk. Help him find the funk. __

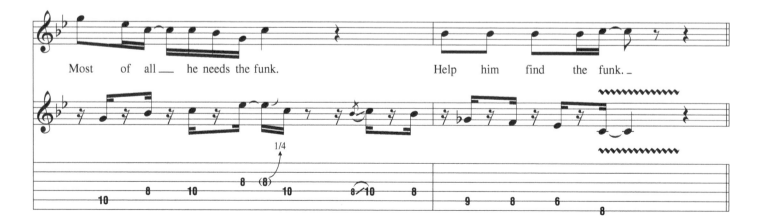

Most of all __ he needs the funk. Help him find the funk. __

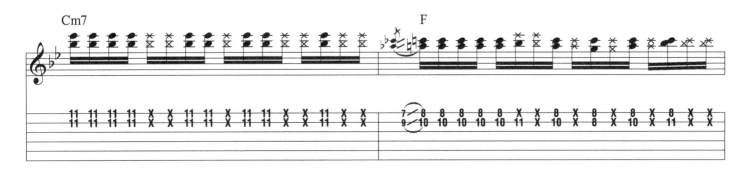

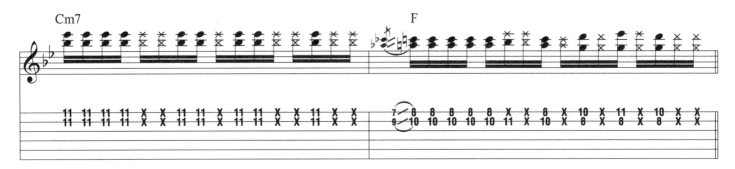

Play 4 times

Flash - light.
Spot - light.
Ne-on light.
Street light.

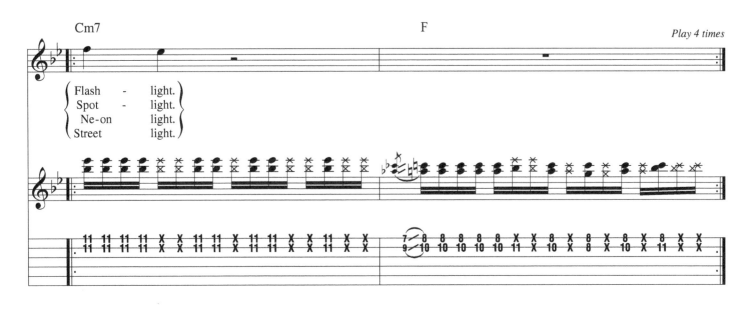

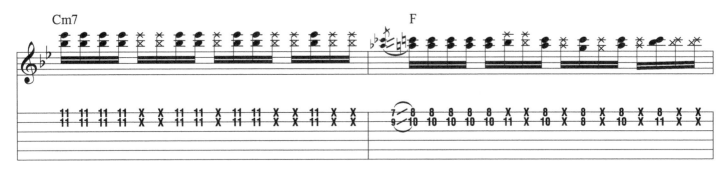

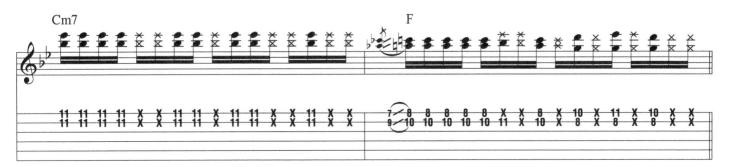

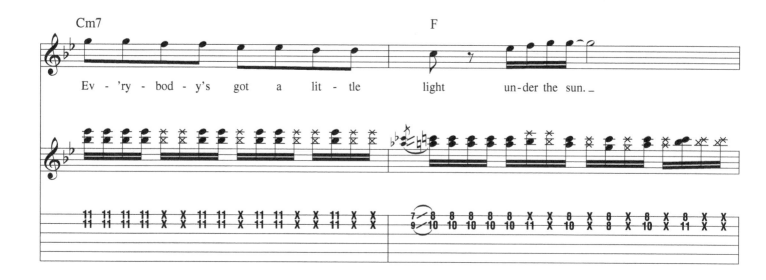

Ev - 'ry - bod - y's got a lit - tle light un-der the sun. _

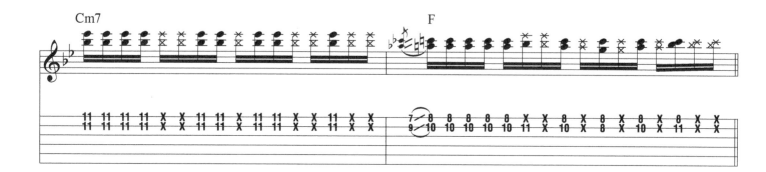

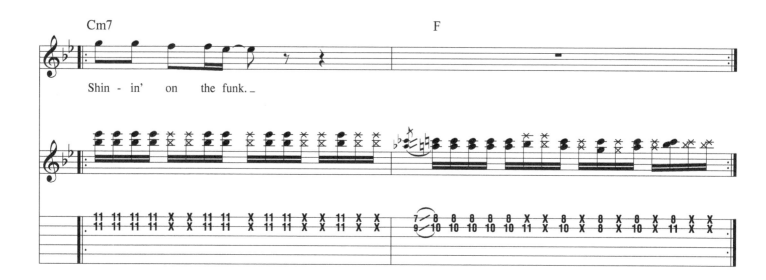

Shin - in' on the funk. _

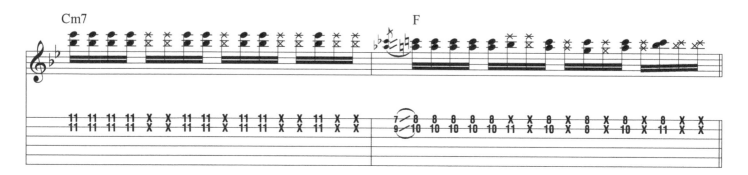

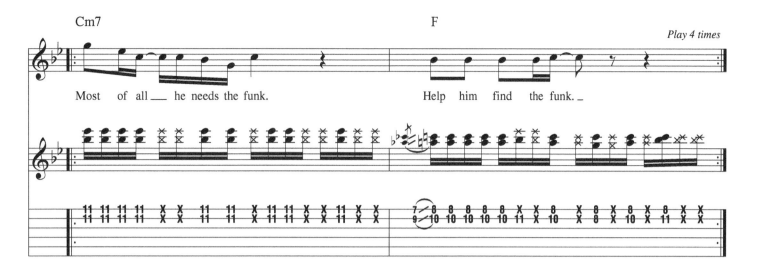

Most of all ___ he needs the funk.

Help him find   the funk. _

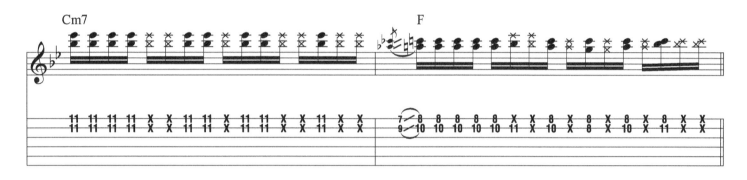

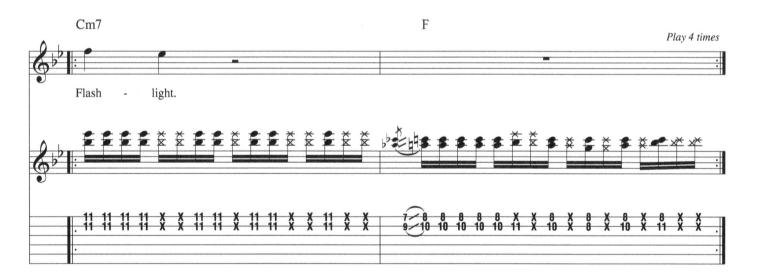

Flash - light.

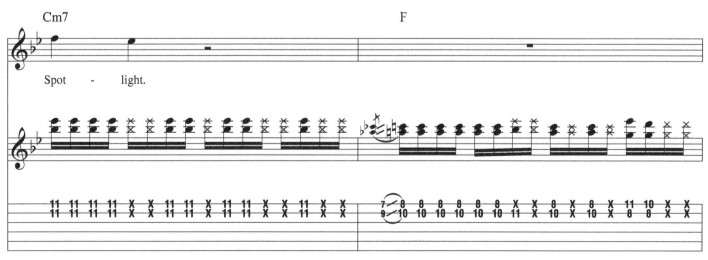

Spot - light.

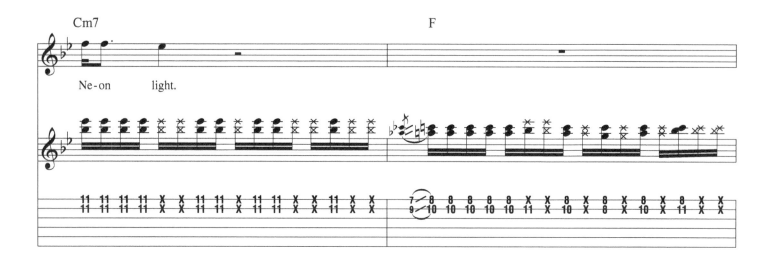

Ne-on light.

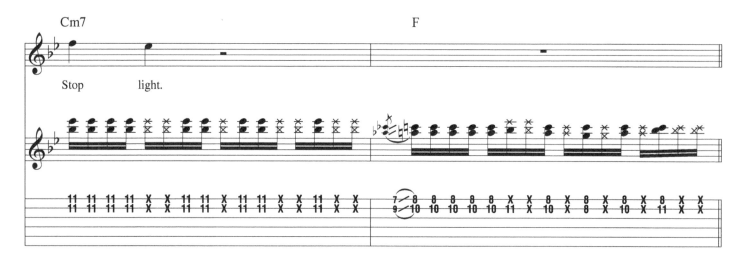

Flash - light.

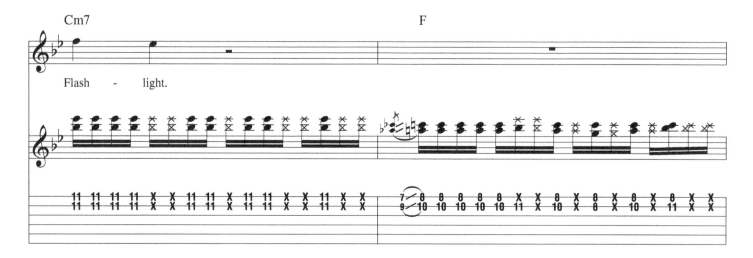

Stop light.

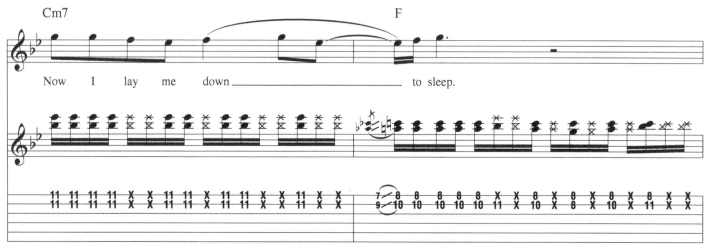

Now I lay me down _____ to sleep.

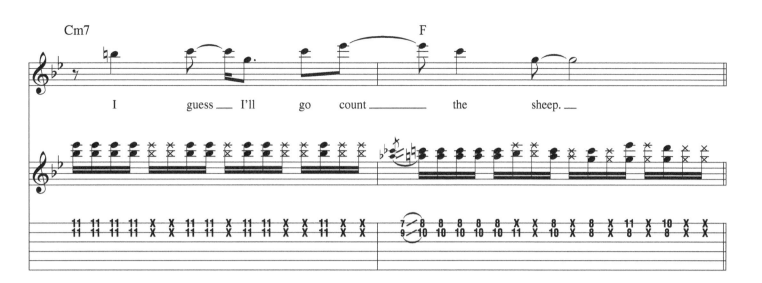

I guess I'll go count the sheep.

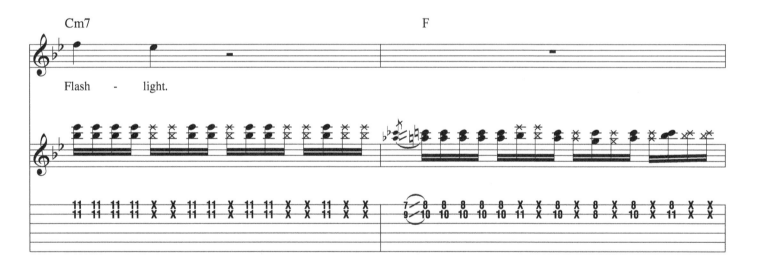

Play 4 times

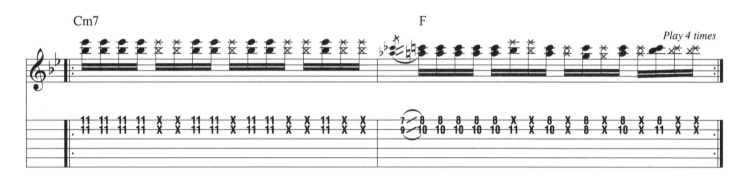

Flash - light.

Day - light.

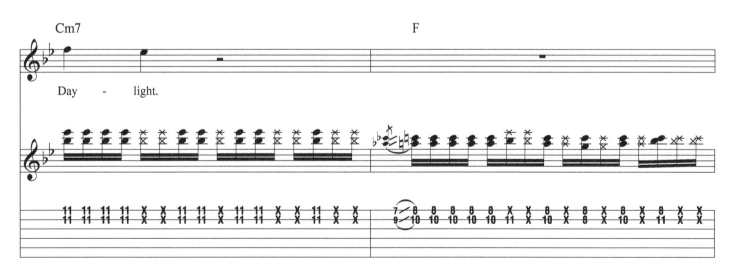

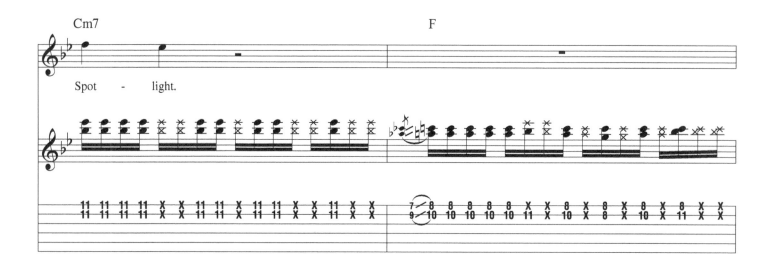

Spot - light.

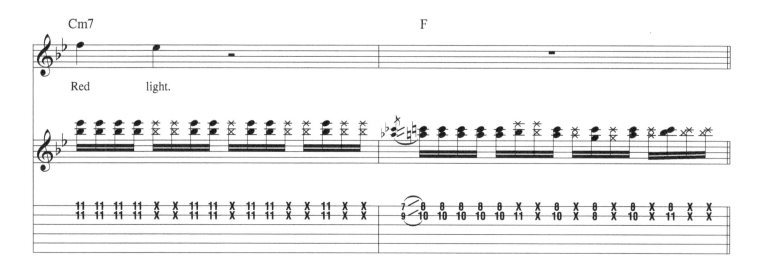

Red light.

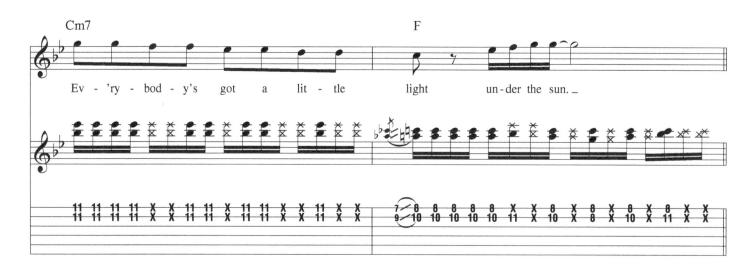

Ev - 'ry - bod - y's got a lit - tle light un - der the sun. _

Repeat and fade

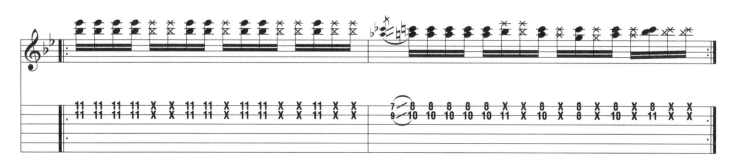

I Just Want to Celebrate

Words and Music by Nick Zesses and Dino Fekaris

Intro
Moderately ♩ = 88

D5

One!   Two!   Three!   Four!

f
w/ dist.

*Key signature denotes D Mixolydian.

N.C.(D7)   G   D

Chorus
N.C.(D7)   G   D

I just want _ to cel - e - brate an - oth - er day _ of liv - in'.

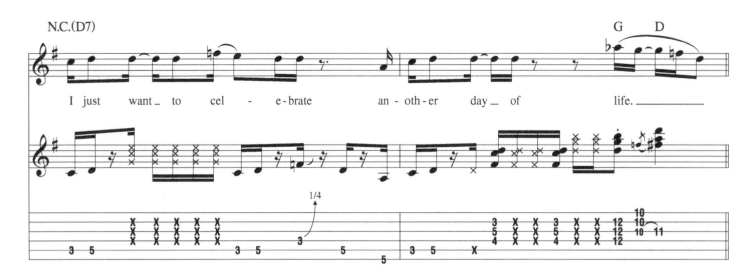

I just want to cel - e-brate an - oth-er day of life.

Verse

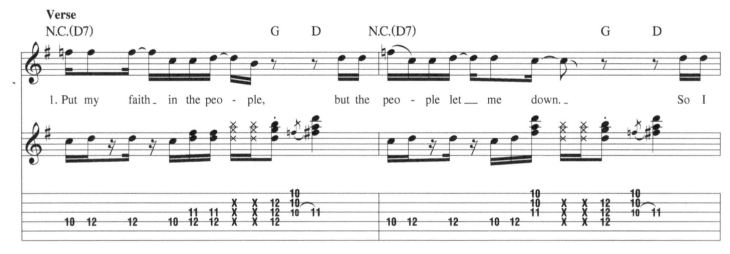

1. Put my faith in the peo - ple, but the peo - ple let me down. So I

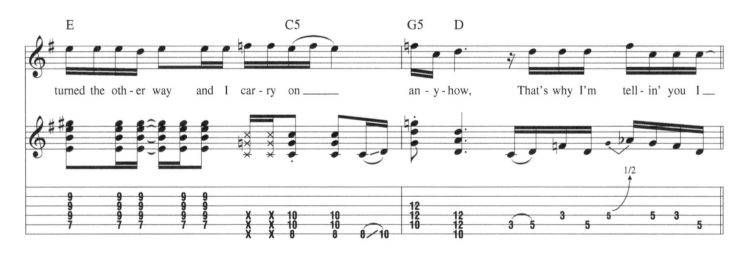

turned the oth - er way and I car - ry on an - y-how, That's why I'm tell - in' you I

Chorus

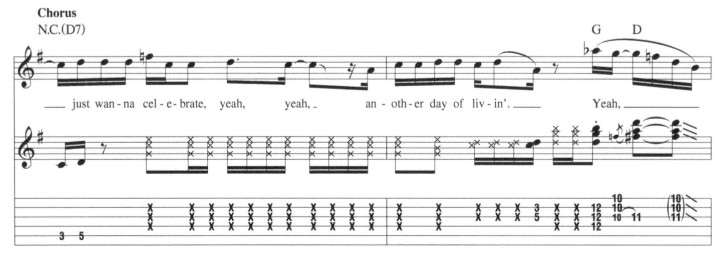

just wan - na cel - e-brate, yeah, yeah, an - oth-er day of liv - in'. Yeah,

I just want␣ to cel - e-brate an-oth-er day␣ of life. _____

Verse

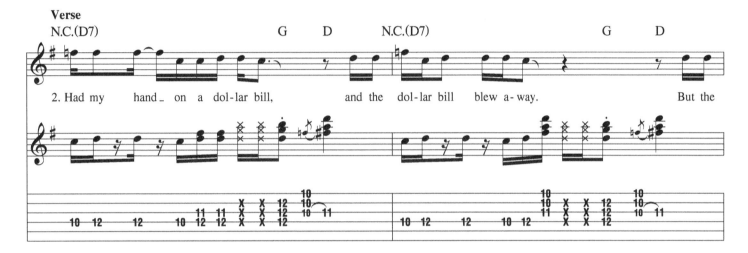

2. Had my hand␣ on a dol-lar bill, and the dol-lar bill blew a-way. But the

sun is shin - in' down␣ on me,␣ and it's here to stay. That's why I'm tell-in' you I␣

Chorus

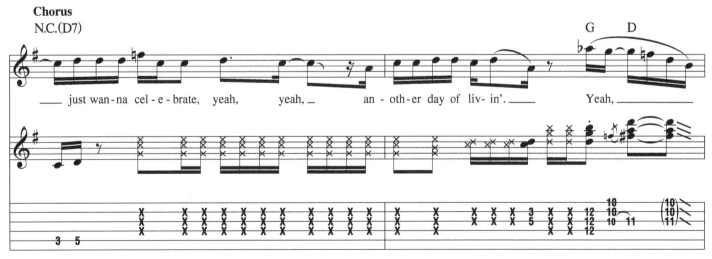

___ just wan-na cel - e-brate, yeah, yeah,␣ an - oth-er day of liv- in'. ___ Yeah, _____

C/D

round   and a - round   and a - round   and a - round   and a -

Guitar Solo

N.C.(D7)

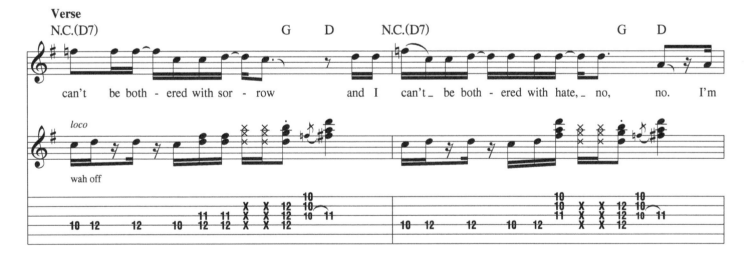

round.   3. Well,   I

w/ wah-wah as filter

Verse

N.C.(D7)   G   D   N.C.(D7)   G   D

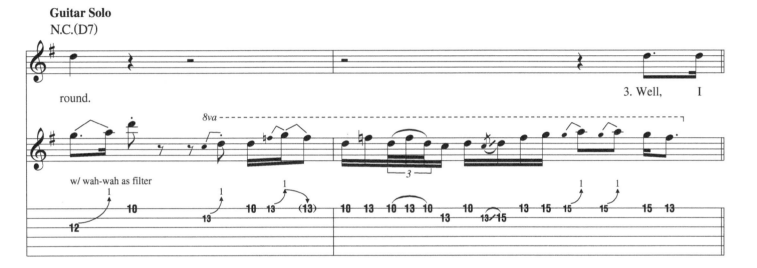

can't   be both - ered with sor - row   and I   can't _ be both - ered with hate, _ no,   no.   I'm

loco

wah off

E   C5   G5   D

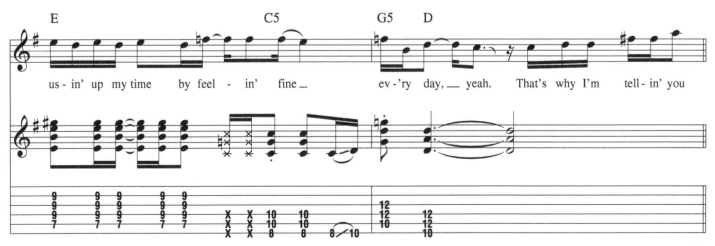

us - in' up my time   by feel - in' fine _   ev - 'ry day, _ yeah.   That's why I'm   tell - in' you

⊕ **Coda**

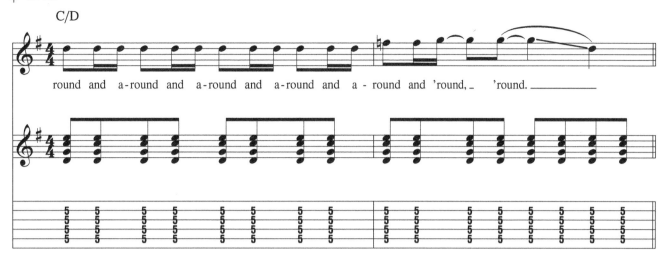

round and a-round and a-round and a-round and a-round and 'round, _ 'round. _____

Interlude

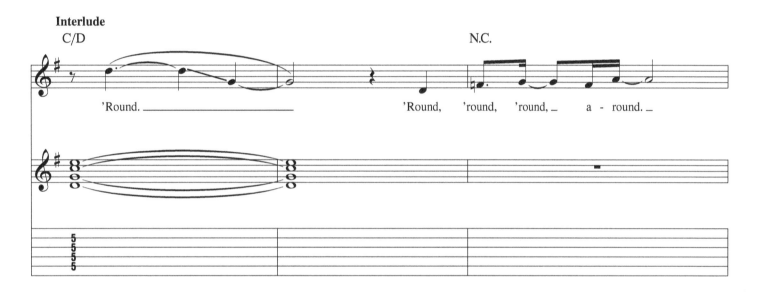

'Round. _____ 'Round, 'round, 'round, _ a - round. _

Gtr. tacet

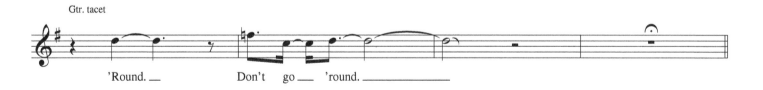

'Round. _ Don't go _ 'round. _____

Drum Break   **Outro**   *Repeat and fade*

I _____ just wan - na cel - e - brate. _____

Funk #49

Words and Music by Joe Walsh, Dale Peters and James Fox

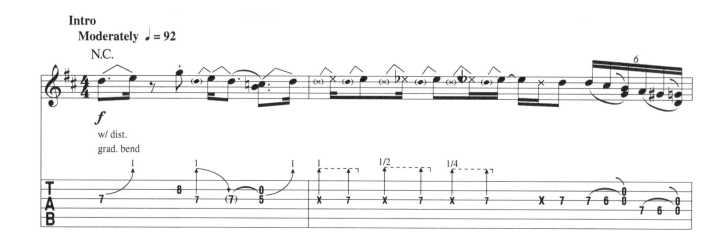

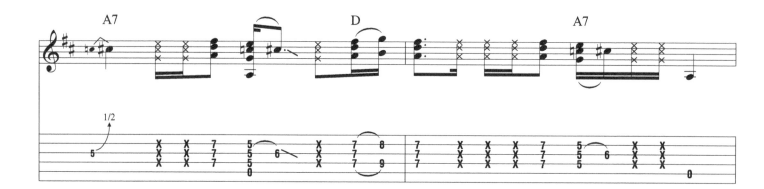

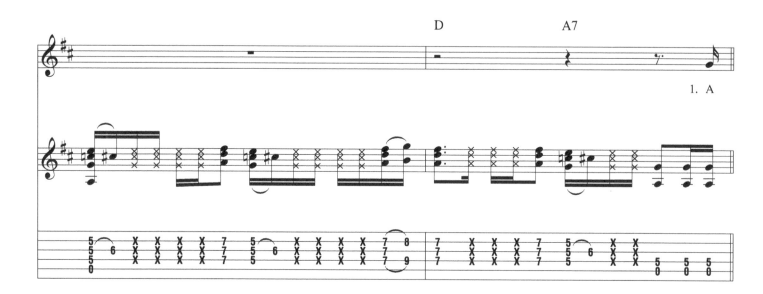

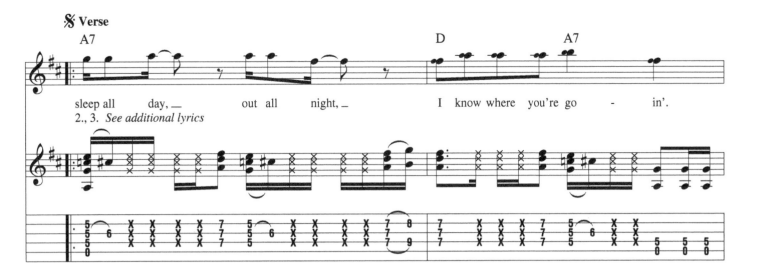

sleep all day, ___ out all night, ___ I know where you're go - in'.

2., 3. *See additional lyrics*

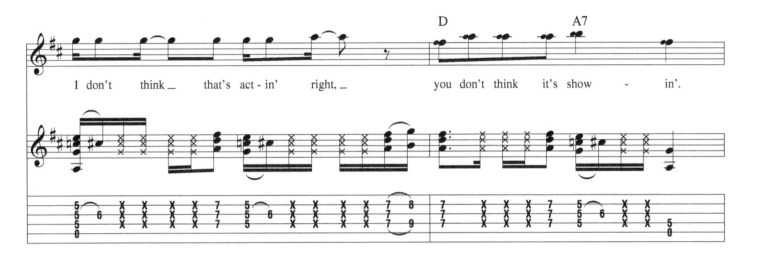

I don't think ___ that's act - in' right, ___ you don't think it's show - in'.

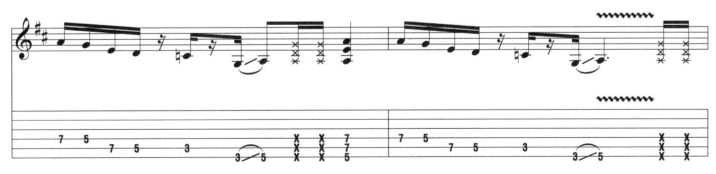

B5

To Coda ⊕

E7♯9

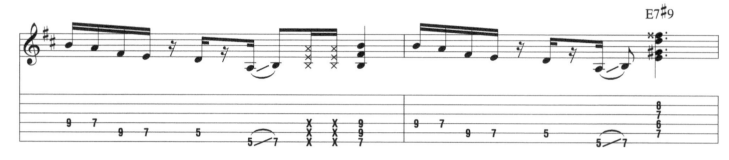

1.

A7   **D**   **A7**

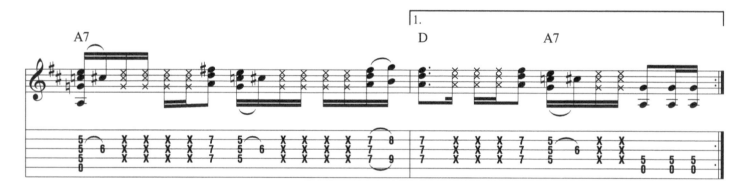

2.

Drum Solo

D   **A7**   **15**

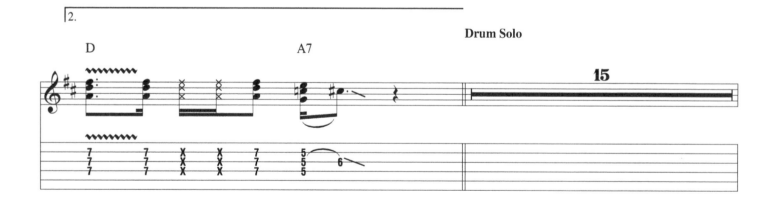

Interlude

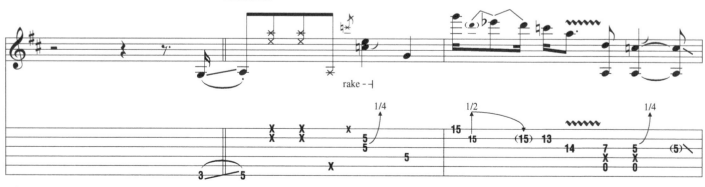

rake

1/4   1/2   1/4

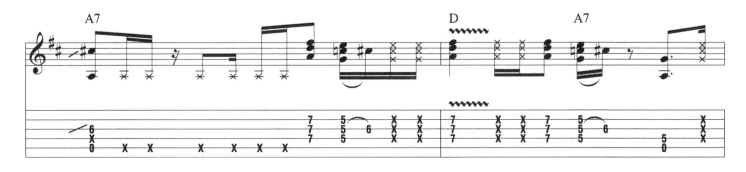

D.S. al Coda

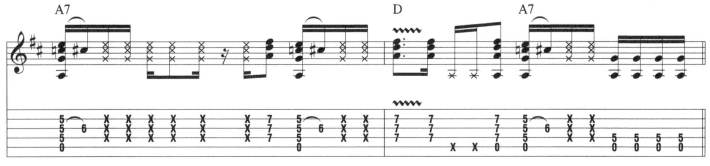

⊕ **Coda**

Outro

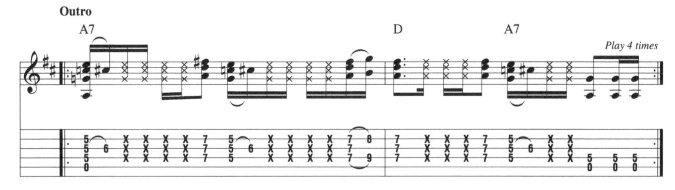

Repeat and fade

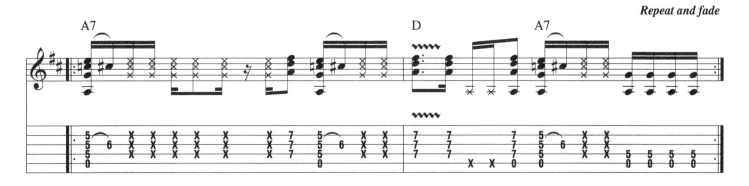

Additional Lyrics

2. A, jumpin' up, fallin' down,
   Don't misunderstand me.
   You don't think that I know your plan;
   What you try'n' to hand me?

3. Out all night, sleep all day,
   I know what you're doin'.
   If you're gonna act this way,
   I think there's trouble brewin'.

It's Your Thing

Words and Music by Rudolph Isley, Ronald Isley and O'Kelly Isley

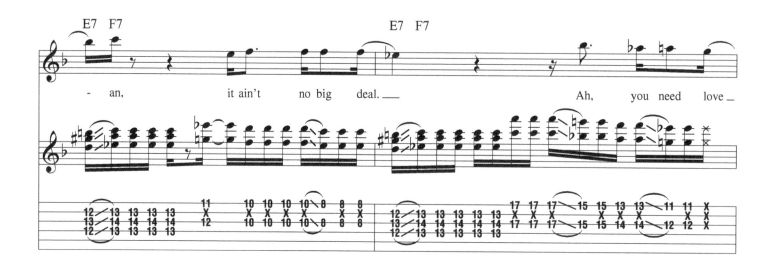

𝄋 𝄋 **Chorus**

I can't tell — ya who to sock it to. — It's — your —

To Coda 2

thing, do what — you wan-na do, now. ___

I can't tell — you who to sock it to. Oh, ___

Interlude

E7 F7   E7 F7

___   yeah.   Al -

right.

Spoken: Lord, have mer- cy.

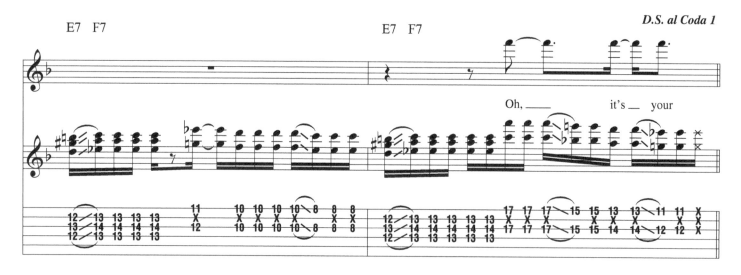

D.S. al Coda 1

Oh, _____ it's _____ your

⊕ Coda 1

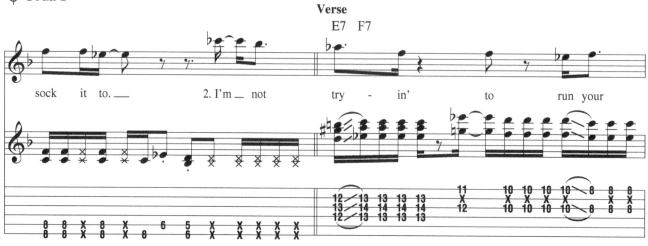

Verse

sock it to. _____ 2. I'm _____ not try - in' to run your

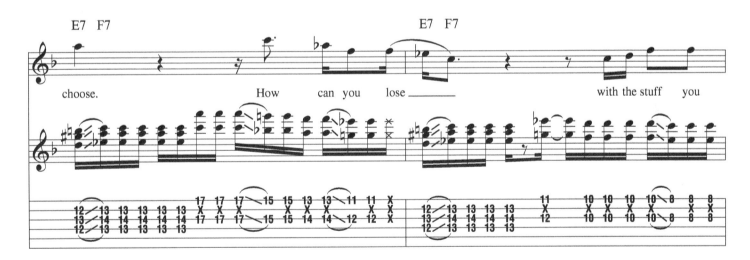

D.S.S. al Coda 2

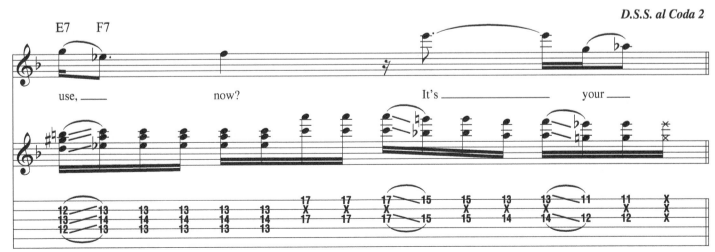

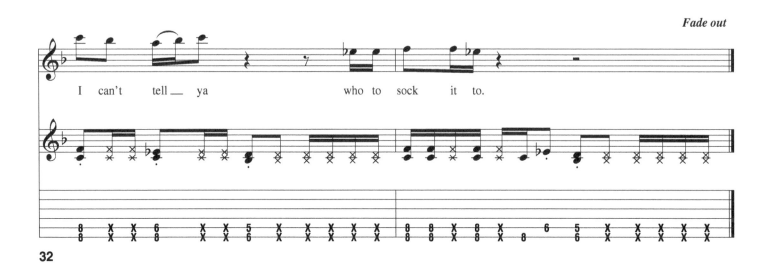

Papa's Got a Brand New Bag

Words and Music by James Brown

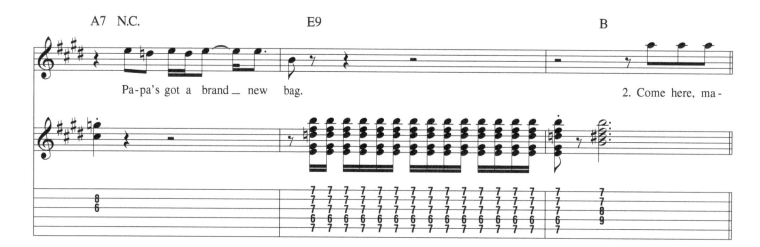

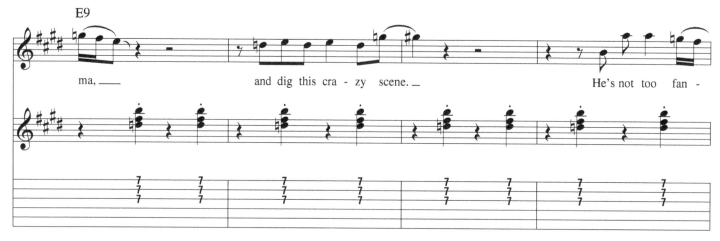

Verse

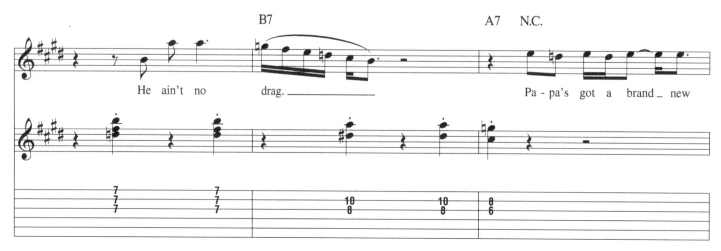

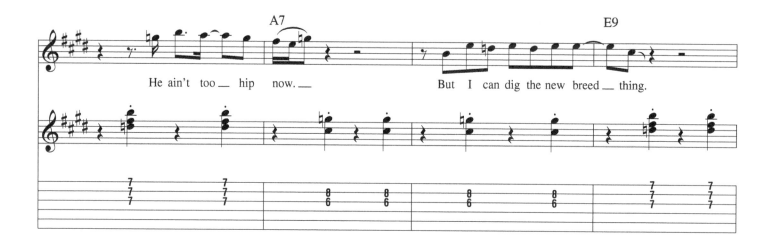

He ain't too — hip now. — But I can dig the new breed — thing.

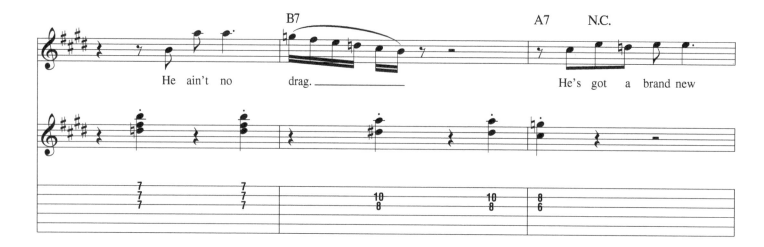

He ain't no drag. — He's got a brand new

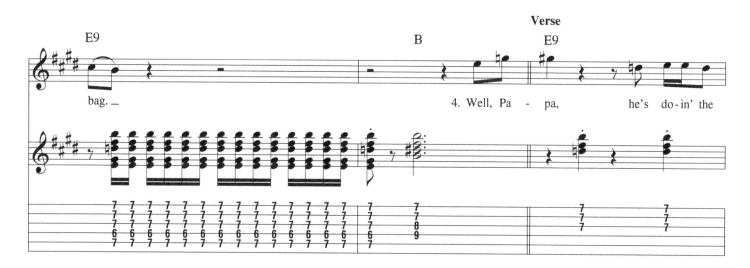

Verse

bag. — 4. Well, Pa - pa, he's do - in' the

jerk. Pa - pa, he's do - in' the jerk. He's do - in' the twist just like —

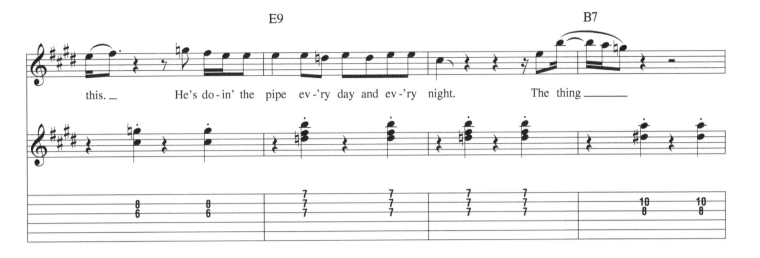

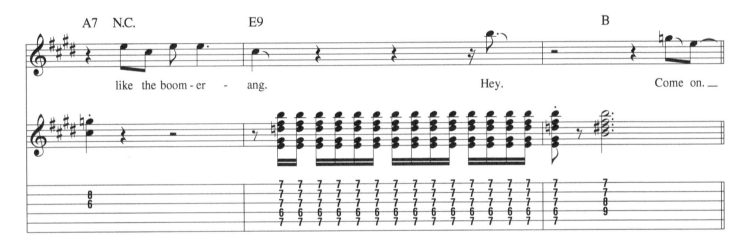

Outro

Le Freak

Words and Music by Nile Rodgers and Bernard Edwards

Chorus
Moderately ♩ = 124

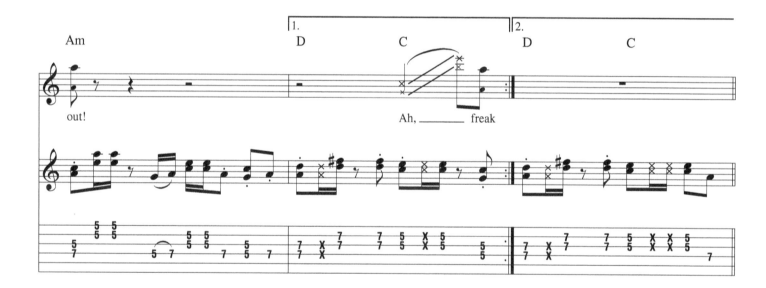

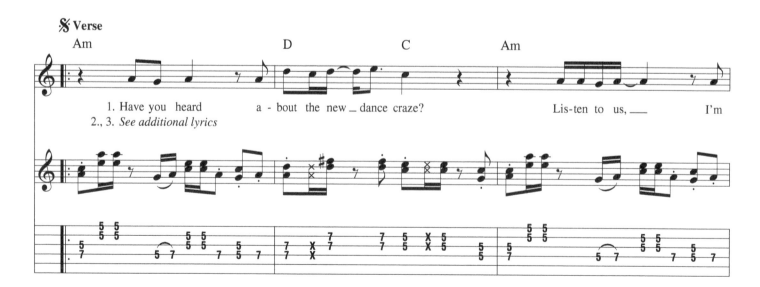

sure you'll be a-mazed. _ Big fun _ to be had by ev-'ry-one. _

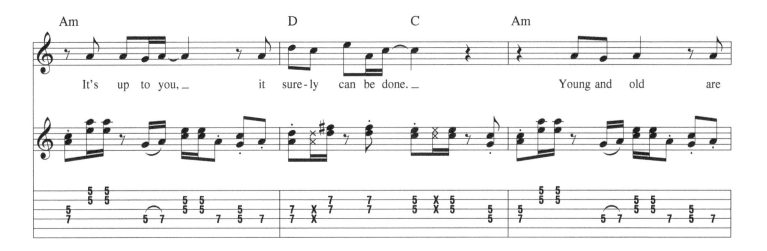

It's up to you, _ it sure-ly can be done. _ Young and old are

2nd & 3rd times, substitute Fill 1

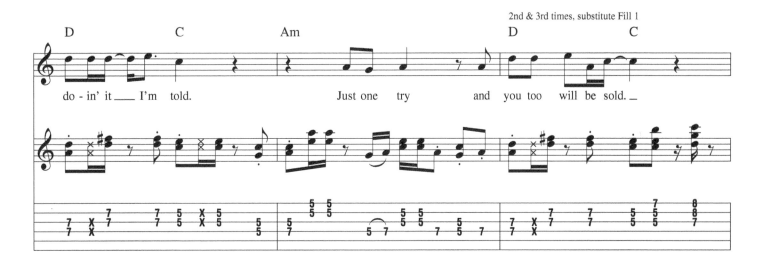

do-in' it ___ I'm told. Just one try and you too will be sold. _

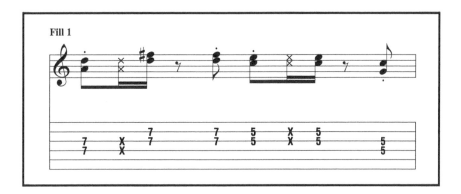

Fill 1

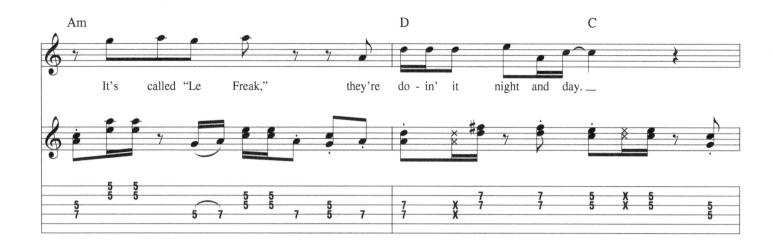

It's called "Le Freak," they're do-in' it night and day. ____

To Coda ⊕

Al-low us, we'll show you the way. ____ Ah, _____ freak

Chorus

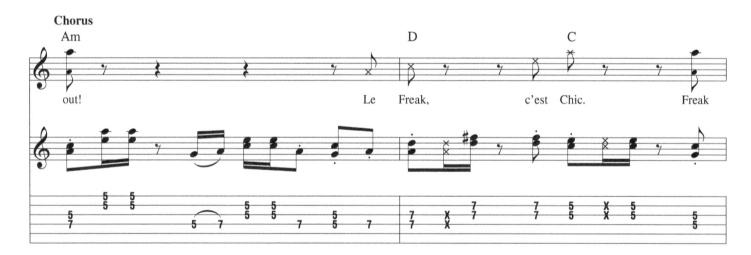

out! Le Freak, c'est Chic. Freak

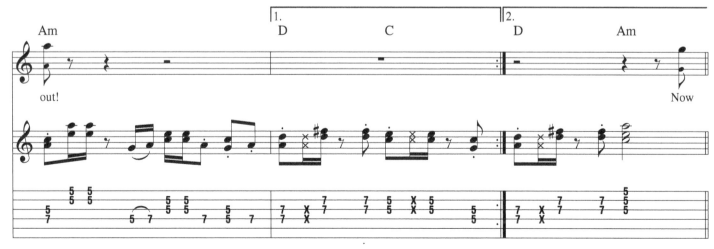

out! Now

Interlude

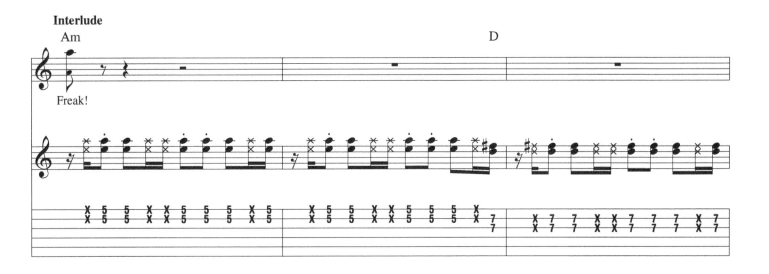

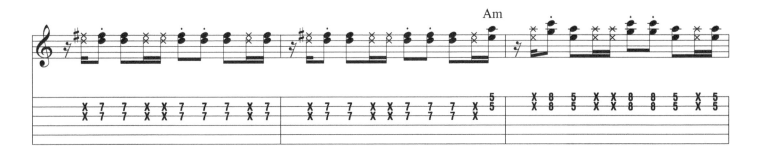

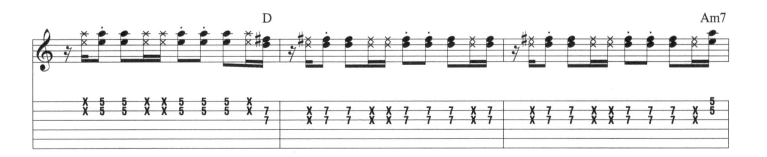

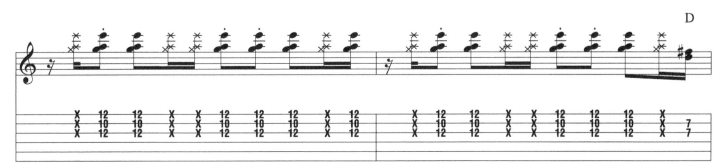

I said, "Freak!" _

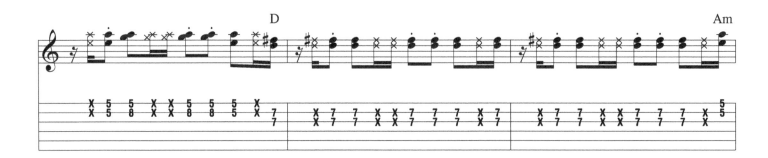

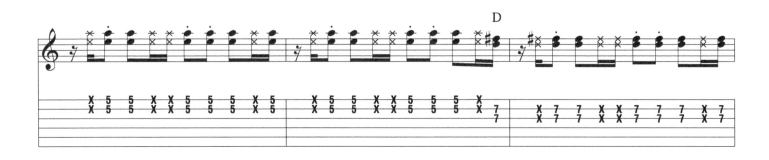

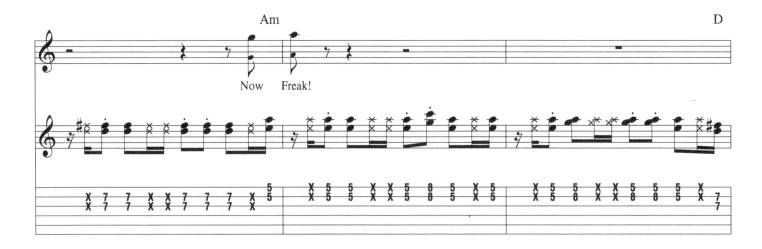

Now Freak!

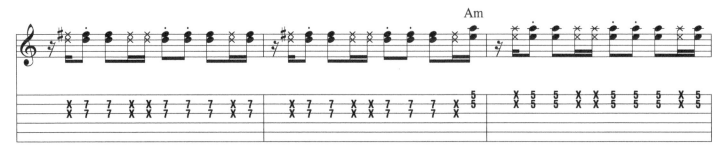

⊕ Coda

Outro-Chorus

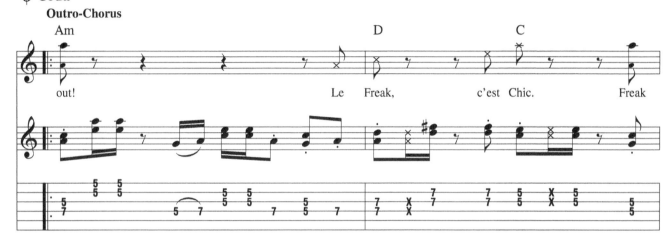

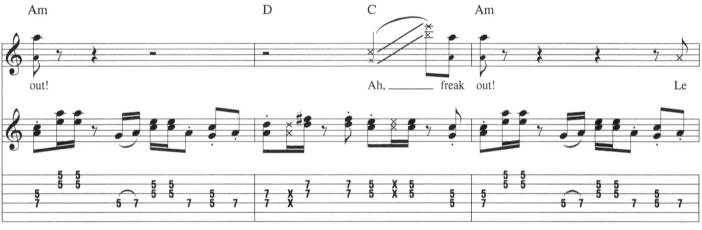

Play 4 times & fade

Additional Lyrics

2., 3. All that pressure got you down,
Has your head spinning all around.
Feel the rhythm, chant the rhyme.
Come on along and have a real good time.
Like the days of stompin' at the Savoy,
Now we Freak. Oh, what a joy.
Just come on down to 54,
Find a spot out on the floor.

Pick Up the Pieces

**Words and Music by James Hamish Stuart, Alan Gorrie, Roger Ball,
Robbie McIntosh, Owen McIntyre and Malcolm Duncan**

Moderate Funk ♩ = 106

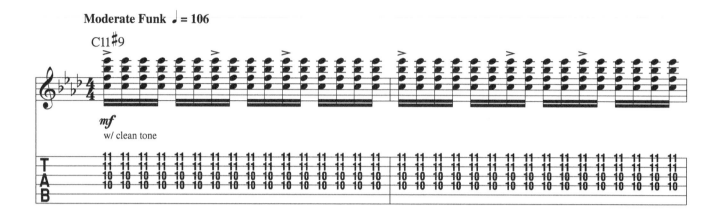

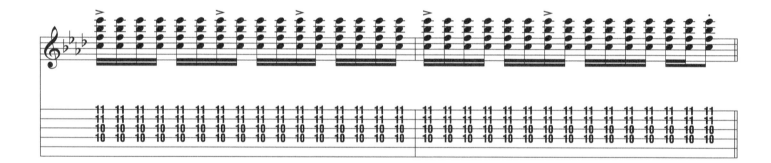

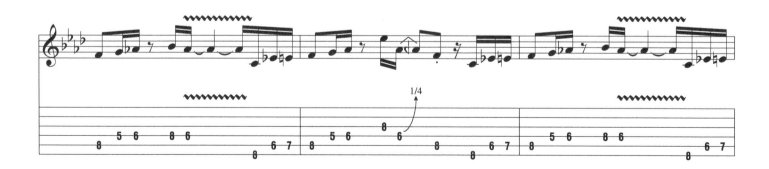

3rd time, To Coda 1 ⊕

4th time, To Coda 2 ⊕

D.S. al Coda 1

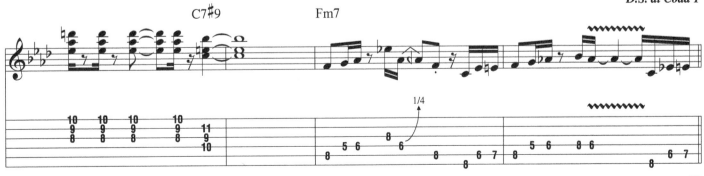

D.S. al Coda 2

⊕ **Coda 2**

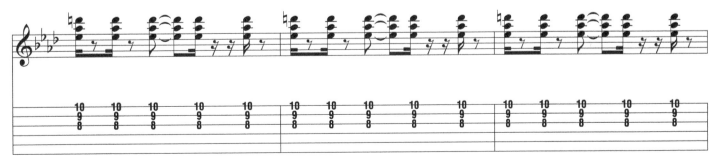

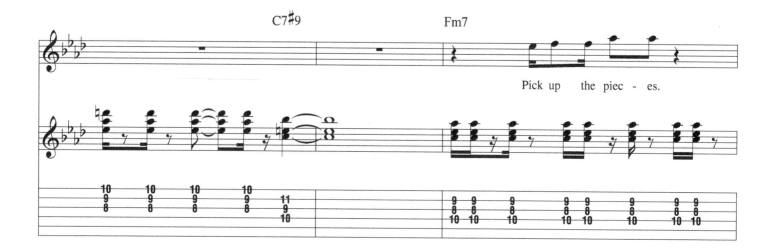

Pick up the piec - es.

Pick up the piec - es.   Pick up the

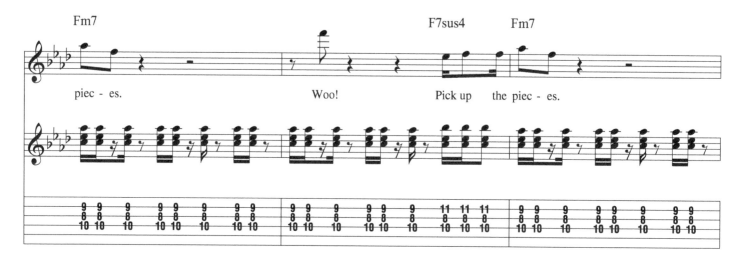

piec - es.   Woo!   Pick up the piec - es.

Ow! _____